THE CASH FACTOR

BY

TRACE REDDICK

Ordering Information: Quantity sales: Special discounts are available on quantity purchases by corporations, associations and others. Orders by U.S. trade bookstores and wholesalers: Please contact Trace Reddick by visiting www.TraceReddickMBA.com

www.DreamStartersPublishing.com

Table of Contents

At Dorado Finance, we facilitate the American Dream. We catalyze business-to-business growth so that your cost is the cost of the opportunity. The fact that we become a crucial instrument in helping dreams live on gives me purpose. I witness on a daily basis just how magical it is to see an entrepreneur do what he or she does best – grow something from nothing.

*When you decide to start a business, you absolutely must have a crystal-clear vision of your future. You need to start smart. By that, I mean you should be prepared and understand what you're getting into. Debt kills dreams. It can ruin your business very quickly, and bankruptcy doesn't always save you from debt. This book is for the entrepreneur who doesn't want to sell his or her soul for debt. It's for the person who wants to grow his or her B2B business on his or her terms. It's for the fighter who is born to keep the dream alive. **The Cash Factor** is more than just a manual. It is the solution.*

-Trace Reddick

Chapter 1

Let Your Customers Capitalize Your Business

First thing: Don't take the bank's money. The way to raise capital isn't by going into debt before you even get off the ground. The sure-fire way to raise capital is by getting your product out there in the hands of your consumers. Let your customers capitalize your business. That's where I come in. My father, Gene, started a small factoring company in El Paso, Texas, in the late 1990s. He was an entrepreneur and I was blessed enough to get that gene, too (no pun intended). My passion in life is business and the American Dream. My purpose is to help others successfully create their own American Dream.

The first rule is do not go and get overleveraged by debt. More often than not, traditional finance lines are determined by faceless humans looking at numbers. Don't get me wrong, numbers are very important, but they don't tell the whole story. You always know someone or multiple 'someones' you can borrow money from. Start with friends and family if you can. Plan and be prepared to prove to them that your business/product (what I call 'your "solution"') is viable

Too many businesses fail before ever getting off the ground because they're in debt before they start or don't stick to 'the plan'. I'll give you a real-life example. I should tell you in advance that I have helped open three restaurants in upper-management roles and watched two of them fail. I hear of and know of similar stories all the time.

There's this restaurant that opened down the street from where I live. As happens when you're hanging around a place for an extended period of time, I started picking up on conversations among the employees and owners. It turns out they were in trouble -- big trouble from the sound of things. From the bits and pieces I put together, it was obvious they had taken out some hefty loans to help finance the restaurant before they weren't even open. I knew I had to help if I could.

I went to talk to them. Turns out the owners were funding this restaurant for their son, whose dream was to be a chef of his own restaurant. They felt they could make a go of the venture and turn it into a family business. Mom had experience in accounting, so they figured they already had a handle on the financial part of the business. That left the fun of planning the restaurant itself.

Despite the son having been *in* the restaurant business, I felt confident they had never actually *started* a business before. In short, they were in trouble. There were financial issues from the get-go. Turns out they had been taking out large loans ($400,000 each) so they could pay their employees and buy the best or nicest of everything. Those employees included 11 high-powered chefs. First, few restaurants hire 11 trained chefs, let alone high-powered chefs. Second, you never take out loans to make your payroll without knowing your business cycles. They were now upside down with heavy debt, and the restaurant wasn't even open yet.

In the midst of this financial meltdown, they were learning a very valuable lesson. Especially their son, who was learning very quickly that working in an established restaurant as a hired-on chef is entirely different from being the owner, operations manager and executive chef. Handling all these titles was not just a little different, but incredibly different. Being the owner of a restaurant and running it in addition to being the chef and creative resource behind the business is exponentially more difficult.

As a result of their inexperience and the debt they had accrued, the restaurant closed without having made it a year. You might think, with mom being an accountant, they would have known and avoided all this. That's what I would have thought, too. It just shows you that even smart people can make mistakes. Their ability to leverage their capital for steady cash flow and business longevity was wiped out by excess payroll.

Here's the thing. When you sit down at a restaurant, get served and enjoy a good meal, it all looks like it happens seamlessly. When you're the hired chef, your time is devoted to creating great meals that wow the guests. You're not focused on the rest of the operational activities going on in the background, so it might look pretty easy to you. But I tell you from experience: That is far, far from it.

According to a study commissioned by Restaurant Startup & Growth (RS&G) magazine, there is a 23 percent failure rate for restaurants within the first year. The study was conducted in Dallas, Texas, which, according to the National Restaurant Association, ranks second in the nation per capita in food spending outside the home. What that means is that one in four restaurants will fail within a year.

I have experience with this, as I wrote above, because in my early 20s I got involved with two investors who wanted to open a couple of restaurants. They wanted to open the restaurants within about 45 miles of each other and within 30 days of each other. Crazy, I know, but we did it. One was in Tupelo, Mississippi, and the other in Oxford, Mississippi. They hired me as the general manager for the Oxford location. They also hired an assistant general manager and executive chef. Combined, the three of us did not have five years of management experience. Not only did *we* not have the right experience, but the guys trying to start the restaurants didn't, either. Just like that, we became a statistic: One of the 23 percent of restaurants that fail. We were in over our heads and headed for failure before we even started.

This experience gave me a good glimpse into the restaurant world and a lot of schooling on just what goes into opening and operating a business in general, and it is not easy. No business is easy.

I have a solution and some pearls for those seeking to level up or start your business-to-business (B2B) business. At Donado Finance, we facilitate that ability to level up and foster explosive growth with zero debt, which I'll dive into later. We're a family business that is in business to help businesses grow and keep on growing.

When you decide to start a business, you absolutely must have a crystal-clear vision of your future. You need to start smart. By that I mean you should start small and grow organically; don't try to start big and fit into shoes that are too large for you. Stick within your means. Perform your service for your customers and let them fund, or capitalize, your business. If you don't, you may find yourself in over your head, and most certainly that will include a financial crisis. Debt kills dreams. It can ruin you very quickly. Bankruptcy doesn't always save you from debt. If you're a sole proprietor, you may file bankruptcy on your business, but that will only transfer the debt over to you personally. Now, not only has your business failed, but your personal finances and credit are on the line.

Let me give you a real-life example of one of my good clients called H&H has a payroll of about $80,000 to $100,000 and growing every week. It is a staffing agency and when its temps/staff signs on, the only thing the temps want and expect is to be paid in full and on time. It's such an obvious and clear expectation from any operating business. These temp staffers will do anything for my client's customers: Sort mail, clean hotel rooms, can processed meat, whatever it is for which they are signing up. Again, the one and only thing they expect in return is to be paid in full and on time. They have about 200-plus employees. As a business owner, that is a lot of mouths and familes depending on you. No pressure, right?

You see the problem? If H&H has to wait the 30 or 60 or 90 days it takes for its customers' payments to come in, it would certainly fall short of meeting its commitment to its employees (inventory, so to speak), the backbone of H&H's

business. H&H would consistently miss payroll obligations and cease to be in business.

The second most-difficult thing for any business is to get the cash across the finish line. No. 1 is to get the signature on the contract, then from there it is to get the cash for your hard work. America is in large part a service-industry country. Many, many businesses can be started without a huge infusion of capital. All you need to do is identify a problem and provide your target customer with a viable solution, invoice them and then sell the invoice to a "factor" like me, so you get immediate payment and can continue to grow. That's where I come in. My company provides our customers like H&H with a viable solution. We buy its invoices as soon as the invoice is issued so it is able to consistently meet its obligations and keep moving forward.

Being a revenue-first-based business, you have options. We lend on assets you may have that you don't even realize, for example, accounts receivables. We can get you cash in your hands faster than a credit card so you're able to do things like re-invest, hire more people for a job, buy another semi-truck to grow your fleet, upgrade to a more robust software system to reduce costs or streamline processes. We facilitate the American Dream. We help you save the money and grow by allowing you to do business first so you can have a bigger tomorrow.

Questions

What is your business?

_____

_____

What problem does your business solve?

_____

_____

_____

How much capital do you need to get the business started or to the next growth stage?

_____

_____

_____

What steps do you need to take to grow your business now and in the future? Have you created a roadmap?

_____

_____

_____

_____

For a number of major companies, if you cant access commercial markets, you cant fund your business. That's a big problem. You can't pay your bills."

Kenneth Chenault

Chapter 2

Know Your Client Base

My first entrepreneurial memory is of when I was 5 years old. I didn't eat any of my Halloween candy that year. I put it in a pillowcase and I went door to door the next day to sell that candy. I mean, what kid wouldn't want more candy? All I wanted for it was $5. Shocker: Nobody wanted to buy the candy from me. Why? Most parents that answered the door knew they had basically just bought the candy a few days before, so they weren't going to buy it back from me. I was only 5 and I didn't understand that at the time. So I just kept going because I wanted what I wanted. I rang what seemed like hundreds of door bells -- and finally got a yes. That's when I got my first sales high and figured out that you can make money doing just about anything. The follow-up (there is always follow-up in business): A few days later the mom of my customer brought the candy back to me and asked for the money back. I sure didn't know my target audience at 5 years old, but I got creative and gave them the money back if they let me play with their Nintendo, which was a big no-no in my household -- and worth way more than $5 to me.

If you want to start a successful, long-lasting business, there are steps to take before you begin. The first thing is to have a crystal-clear vision of your future. You need a strategic plan. You need to know what your business is going to be doing, what problem you're solving, how you can do it better or are more valuable than the next guy, and identify your buyer or target audience. If your first thought is, 'How do I figure that out?', you're not alone. It's going to take a lot of work to plan your business before you even start. Your target audience is the client base that your company wants to serve. They share similar characteristics, wants and needs. To get started, you need to learn everything you can about them and collect information. Log this information into a customer relationship management program (CRM). I recommend Hubspot. It's free and can scale very easily with you. Next, build a revenue model by figuring out how you are going to generate dollars for the service or widget you offer.

A lot of people who want to start a business don't even know who they are going after. Here's a good example: I was consulting for a start-up in Chicago and when I asked what it does, the company's answer was "everything." Then when I asked who the customers are or should be, they were not able to identify the characteristics of a company that would be seeking the service my client offered. My client and I spent a lot of time figuring out who his customers could be so that we could determine how to generate leads.

There was a famous company that started making shoe inserts to relieve foot pain. When it started out, it targeted the working person -- the guy standing on his feet all day in the warehouse or on the construction site or the guys working long hours in the steel mills or the person manning the cash register in a grocery store. The inserts provided extra support and cushioning to relieve the foot pain and even back pain these people experienced from spending hours and hours on their feet. This company wanted to make the work day more comfortable for these people and it made a great and successful effort to win the attention of this audience.

Here is what the company found out. While analyzing demographics of consumers buying its foot pads, it discovered there was a large population of athletes purchasing the pads, as well. It turned out that the athletes were getting a huge amount of relief when they used the inserts in their shoes while practicing. Initially, the company missed out on a whole market segment because it looked only at a very narrow segment of its market. There are so many people out there that experience foot pain. The company soon realized this.

There are things you need to know before you try to start a business. There is a process to go through before you begin building your business if you want to be successful. These are the steps you need to take:

- **Know your business**

- **Identify your customer**
    - Who is your target audience?

- **Collect information**
    - What are your customers' needs?
    - How would they use your product?
    - How do you add value to the buyer?

- **Learn all you can about your customer**
    - Know you are not your customer.
    - Know and understand your target audience before you try to grow your audience.

- **Leverage a neutral party to verify your vision**
    - Make sure the numbers work. Work you plan backwards. Is the financial model sustainable?
    - Think lawyer here. Know what can go wrong before something does wrong. Legal advice is cheaper before you find yourself needing an

attorney to save your business. Notice I said 'verify' not 'validate'. Its ok when someone tells you you're crazy.

I have a personal example of how you can become incredibly successful by following the right process. H&H, like I mentioned before, is headed for $8 million in revenue this year. Again, the business is a staffing agency. And it is a very fine example of achieving the American dream.

The owners of H&H are legal Mexican immigrants. When they came to this country, they experienced first-hand how temp agencies worked because that is where they started. In their time spent working for these agencies, they saw how their bosses were doing things very wrong. They identified a need and an understanding of how they could offer the same solution themselves, but in a better way. So they gave up their hourly jobs to start their own agency. Sure, they work 80-hour weeks now. However, they are so much happier, and they are making more money than they ever thought possible.

The secret to their success is that they knew their client base, the types of businesses that need someone to come in and tackle tasks like sorting mail, filing or food prepping and manufacturing. H&H leveraged the right businesses. It knew the problems faced by its target consumer. H&H had a workforce to supply to the targeted businesses. In short, they understood the problem and had the right solution. Before they started, they had a strategic plan.

As a factor, Dorado knows and understands our clients, like H&H, thoroughly. We know them at their core. We understand the reason our clients leverage our service and how they will use it. We know how often our services will be needed. Since we are a relatively small factoring firm, we have a key competitive advantage over larger factors because we can respond to our clients more quickly and be more flexible. We work with people. Our clients become part of our family. We have their same values and we have walked in their shoes.

When you start a business, you need hard evidence to support your ideas of how that business is going to bring you success. You need to leverage all the data you have available to be able to predict how your target audience behaves, and if your product or service will hit the mark. There are many and multiple ways to collect data using today's technology. The internet provides an unimaginable amount of free and for-sale information right at your fingertips.

It may take time to determine and define your target audience. But it will be time well spent. Focusing on who your audience is will uncover the most effective way for you to market your product or service. Knowing and understanding your target audience allows you to align your services with their expectations.

Questions

Have you developed a written strategic plan?

_____

_____

_____

What does your ideal client look like?

_____

_____

_____

How does your solution address the market's wants and needs?

_____

_____

_____

How will you continue to adapt to the evolving needs of your customers and your industry?

_____

_____

_____

_____

"Rule 405: Always know your client."

Greg Adams

Chapter 3

Add Value

You've got to be in business to be able to help somebody else be in business. Why are you selling what you're selling? To be successful, you must have a relationship with your customer that benefits both you and your customer.

In a past life, after the restaurants, I started a lapel-pin business. When I started selling lapel pins, I was one of maybe five people that did this in my tiny niche. I had only two competitors in my specific niche market, which was concerts for a specific genre of music. Here's how it went: I went into the concert with a bunch of pins in my pockets and walked out with an easy $1,000+ cash in my pocket after less than two hours.

It cost me only about a $1 each to make these pins, but I was charging $15 each. That's a lot of profit. Think about it. I was selling somewhere between 50 to 70 pins and making close to a thousand bucks cash each show. Subtract the $50 to $70 I spent to have the pins made plus some money for flights to get to the shows, and maybe some lunch, and I was making a great profit. I knew who my customers were. I knew what they liked, why they would buy from me rather than someone else. I knew who would buy from me before that person even knew I was in the building. As you can imagine, it didn't take long for other people to catch on.

When other entrepreneurial types started hearing about my success and the success of my friendly competition, they began to realize how lucrative this business could be. There were really no barriers to getting into the market. There was little-to-no overhead for a product that turned a quick, easy and pretty good profit. So as you would expect, others quickly entered the market, and it got very competitive and new entrants grew quickly due to the favororable environment.

What this did for me was to make me pay attention to how I was marketing my product. I became very aware and much more conscious of my business. I started taking a look at how I was doing business and asking myself if there was enough value in my product to justify what I was charging. Was I charging too much? Should I be charging more? I came up with these answers:

1. Longevity: I had been around a long time.

2. Customer base: I had already established my presence in the market.

3. Reputation: I had a good reputation and the respect of my customers

4. Portfolio: I carried a diverse product line that included some of the most popular designs.

5. Online presence: I had a good website, and it was easy for people to view my product and order it.

All that added up to value. In short, I had a winner. I decided that what I was charging for my product was just right. That's when I decided it was time to integrate into the wholesale (backward integration),then further to the manufacturing side, of the pin business in order to gain a strategic advantage over my competitors and control the market. I've always disliked the price game and as a result, I consistently have to make sure that my value proposition is strong and air-tight.

You may be wondering what I mean by backward integration. Backward integration allows a company to expand and take control of its suppliers. It's a kind of vertical move, actually. It's generally done through acquisition or merger with a supplier, and by doing so, the company achieves a leg up on its competitors.

There are several benefits to backward integration. The primary, of course, is cost reduction. Think about this: When you acquire or merge with a supplier, you are no longer subject to its operational policies and terms and conditions. The control of your product from design through sale is now in your hands. You are free to implement changes that can improve efficiency and overall operations, resulting in healthy cost reductions. You can even sell excess capacity (think private labels) to your competitors, so you're still making money.

You are also in a position to create your own branding that sends a consistent and targeted message to your customers focused on their wants and needs. From initial design to final production to getting your product into the hands of your customer, you have total control over the manufacturing processes and quality of the end product. You no longer have to seek out vendors or contractors with the skill sets you need to produce your product. You have direct access to these resources. Total control of your product creates greater customer satisfaction and brand loyalty, and increases revenue.

When you buy or merge with a supplier and create a new company, you acquire access to a larger and previously untapped market. When I expanded and got into wholesaling and manufacturing, I found I had a whole new customer base I could tap into. It opened doors to partnering with clients that were supplying to their customers, a market that was previously out of my reach. All of this put me in the lead over my competitors while increasing my revenue at the same time.

The takeaway here is that knowing your value can open you up to new opportunities that help propel you forward into greater success. When I took a good look at my product, I was able to better understand its value and conclude that it was priced appropriately for its value. But knowing the value of my product did a lot more than that. It gave me the opportunity to backward integrate into wholesaling and manufacturing. From there I was able to take complete control of producing my product from start to finish. I lowered my costs, leveraged my position in my current market, advanced into a previously untapped market and realized a positive impact on revenue.

If you feel like you're being undervalued, do not forget the power of walking away. Look at negotiation strategies that involve walk-away power. It can be really powerful when used tactfully.

Questions

Do you know the value of your product right now?

_____

_____

Is your pricing where it needs to be?

_____

_____

What key values can you list that justify your pricing?

_____

_____

_____

_____

Now that you understand the value of your business, how can you gain an advantage over your competitors?

_____

_____

_____

_____

_____

"The bitterness of poor quality remains long after the sweetness of low price is forgotten"

Benjamin Franklin

Chapter 4

Solve a Problem

When you start a business, you should be solving a problem; selling a solution. Doesn't matter what it is. It could be being a driver, cellular data card supplier, a real estate post-maker, a customs warehouse or even cutting-edge technology for the advancement of prenatal imaging. Every business solves a problem for someone. Restaurants feed people and provide an atmosphere where you can enjoy a meal. A fast-food place is there for when you're on the run and don't have the time to sit down. Shoe stores provide comfortable footwear so your feet don't hurt. Cell phone services provide phones and air time so you don't miss important calls. Every successful business solves a problem.

So you already know that our company does just that. We factor. That is, we buy an asset on the accounting ledger (invoices due or accounts receivables) from companies that are facing stunted growth or cash-flow problems associated with waiting 30, 60 or 90 days to get payment. Receiving money promptly from Dorado Finance or any factor allows our clients to realize their revenue instantly so they can continue to grow operations or other aspects of my clients' business. They can then focus on meeting its their company's obligations to their customers and growing their business. We solve their cash-flow problems that are caused by invoicing issues and delayed payments. We prevent them from having to take out a high-interest loan (debt) to keep operating. We solve their cash-flow problem. We collect their invoices. Sometimes we even teach our clients how to invoice their clients for faster payments.

Thinking of starting a business? Think you have an good idea? Just having an idea for a business is not enough. Your business needs to provide a solution and your passion in life should be to use your solution to make your customers' business better. However, before you can know what that is, you must first identify the problem. Because you have chosen a specific product or service to bring to market, you already have a pretty good idea of the customer you are targeting. Defining and validating the customer's problem, then determining how you're going to execute your solution, is next. This is the most important step to getting your business off the ground -- the method and manner you execute your solution in the marketplace.

All successful businesses solve a problem, right? But know that whatever problem you think you're going to solve, there is possibly somebody already doing it. That doesn't mean there aren't better ways to solve the problem. People are always looking for a better way to do things. So you have to ask yourself, "What/how am I going to offer that's better?"

Solving problems is what excites entrepreneurs. Those with a particluar mindset can take their idea and make it into a reality. I think it's really what drives them. Starting a business takes hard work and people think you're crazy. It's not always easy to have a passion to solve a problem. Generally speaking, the odds are against you…but the odds of being born a human is even higher so you're already ahead of the game. It's difficult to find a need that hasn't been filled or a market that has yet to be discovered. You have to convince your target audience that what you have to offer is worth what you are asking them to spend. How will it improve their lives? What will do it for them that hasn't been done before? How will it be done?

Before you put a lot of time and money into your idea, identify what problem it solves and how viable it will be within your means. If you think it's a viable solution, investigate whether it will have longevity. Talk to potential customers. Ask someone who is already in the industry and has some expertise with what you want to do. Even approach random strangers or businesses and ask them questions. Of course, use tact and approach the situation with transparancy. I am trying to say that information is everywhere. Where is the industry headed? We live in a volatile time. Things are rapidly changing around us. What you might be thinking of today as a problem you can solve may not be bea problem in the future, or perhaps your solution will be obsolete.

If you want to succeed, your product or service has to fill a need that isn't being met. You have to prove to your market that your solution is worth spending money on.

Questions

What business have you, or are you, thinking about starting?

_____

_____

Describe the problem you intend to solve.

_____

_____

_____

_____

_____

What solution will your product or service provide?

_____

_____

_____

_____

_____

Is the solution viable in the long-term? What might impact the lifespan of your solution in the marketplace?

_____

_____

"Someone's sitting in the shade today because someone planted a tree a long time ago."

Warren Buffet

Chapter 5

Build Deep Relationships

Every business relationship must be beneficial to both parties. By that, I mean it's about benefiting each other. A relationship has to benefit you and it has to benefit your client. Again, it's solving problems and being in business to help other businesses be in business.

I've grown my network and book of business because of the relationships I've cultivated with my clients and anyone I meet. Dorado's clients are mostly in the early/raw stages of the supply chain. Our reputation travels by word of mouth. In fact, in more than 20 years, we have spent only $600 on marketing. The relationships we have built with our clients are everything to the success of the business.

It is incredibly important that you cultivate and nurture sincere and honest relationships with your clients, business partners and community members. Communicate with them. Keep them in the know. Show them they are important to you. Your relationships with your business partners are the most important assets you have and play a critical role in your success. When you enter into an alliance with this mindset, you are already creating a deep relationship right from the start; there's a known interdependency already established in your mind. Hopefully your client is aware and recognizes this, as well.

People who are passionate and really good at what they do inherently understand this. They know the value of their network and clients, not to mention their clients' products and services. It's about partnering with your clients. You are their partner in business. Whether it's providing them with a product they use or a service like buying invoices, you are an essential component of their business. You are helping them operate efficiently and effectively so that they generate a profit by offering their customers a solution.

Here's a good example of how businesses solve problems and partner to help each other: Say there is a tortilla factory in partnership with a trucking company that delivers the delicious tortillas to local restaurants. The trucking company plays a critical role in the success of the tortilla factory. If the truck doesn't arrive on time to pick up the tortillas and then deliver them to the restaurants on time, it jeopardizes the tortilla factory's business. The factory's reputation with its clients is dependent on the trucking company honoring and executing its obligations. If the tortillas don't arrive on time, the restaurant won't have them to sell, and then the restaurant has unhappy customers. The restaurant's reputation is dependent on the good relationship between the tortilla factory and delivery truck. And so on. Good relationships in business are critical.

Here's an example of how a relationship I cultivated not only helped the company I was working for but followed me into future business endeavors: When I was involved in an Inc 500 telemedicine software business I worked at and helped start, I disobeyed a direct order from my CEO to forward all the international prospects to him. I had a history of international business success and international business really gets me excited, so I made a calculated decision to ignore his directive and began talking to this prospect from Saudi Arabia myself. I worked hard and I nurtured that relationship to the point where this prospect was ready to make a cash investment in our company to manufacture a service that was desperately needed in his country. But here's the kicker -- the relationship I built and nurtured with this customer turned out to be much more important to me. Fast-forward a couple years down the road, after I left the software company, this prospect became one of my most engaged investors in a medical-cannabis-related venture in Canada.

I don't recommend disobeying your boss. It may backfire for you in a big way, but that's really not the point of my story. My point is that the business relationships you have now are not always tied soley to the business you are in currently. Good client relationships are lasting and, leveraged correctly, will certainly help you grow. People want to see other people they know and like meet their goals. These deep relationships you develop and nurture with your clients will follow you down the line.

When we built our website in 2015,our business gained a relationship with one of our best clients today. In fact, more than just that one client. The rest of our clients, including H&H, came to us from referrals by that one client. Other than that time on Google AdWords, we haven't spent one single dollar on marketing or auto-finance.

Later on, let's say your business isn't working. Guess what? When you've got deep relationships with your clients. you are able to leverage your network and their networks for whatever is next. Maybe it's time to pivot. Maybe you've grown to a point where you have to adapt and your service is no longer relevant. That's when you can leverage those deep relationships to see what they''veexperienced in their worlds so you can be ahead of the curve. When your in these deep lasting relationships, there's open communication.

That is essential: Communicate. Always communicate with your partners in business. Inform them about your business wins. You don't need to brag but an informal email to your list to ask them how they are and inform them how you're doing is a great way to stay on the radar and relevant. Ask them about their successes. People love to talk about themselves. It doesn't have to be a long dissertation. Quick emails with snippets of what's going on are sufficient. They don't take a lot of time, but they keep the communication flowing (always look for opportunities to identify and deploy your solution).

Ask for help when you need it. The flip side is it's important to offer help when you see others need it. Perhaps you saw a post by someone in your network that isn't doing well. Reach out to them; it's not about just talking. Relationships are two-way and give-and-take. To keep them going, you have to participate at all times. This goes beyond business, too. I'm sure you have had people come and go from your life that don't value relationships. Weed out the people that don't value relationships. They do not serve you.

I suspect you know atleast two people that failed at a business venture or position because they didn't treat others appropriately. It may be safe to say that they forgot that a good relationship can be a major lifeline when needed. But if you don't treat others well, the relationships will go bad and you will lose that lifeline. I've seen this happen many times in the venture capital world. I am not talking about theory here; I've had to cut people off in my own life.

One of the best lessons I learned growing up was to never, ever burn bridges. I got into the cannibis industry with a venture capitalist I met in Florida. We were going to buy 52 percent of a medical cannabis operation in its infancy for $30 million. But at the last second, a publicly traded company from Canada came in and started throwing around lawsuits as a delay tactic of the acquisition. It was already over-priced so everyone backed out.

In my mind, the venture capitalist just didn't understand the value of a good relationship. I think in his mind, he valued relationships more than anybody. But what he forgot about was the people making him his money. And it wasn't only about having relationships with the people, with the money, his clients. This was about the people that were operating inside his business -- the foot soldiers, if you will.

As a result of my realization that this guy didn't get it, I quit and burned the bridge. Three days later, the rest of the sales and marketing team walked out. The only reason they stuck it out three more days was because he led them to believe he was going to pay them all a commission. When it came in, it was an insulting figure. He demonstrated unequivocally to them that his sales team...the only revenue center of his business was not important, so they dropped him like a hot potato. The point: You have to take care of your people, not just your clients. If you take care of your people, they'll take care of you and you'll be successful. Treat them badly and you'll lose your greatest assets.

I'd asked this same VC what his biggest mistake had ever been. He told me that Google had wanted to buy the business he and a partner owned, but Google wanted them to move to the Silicon Valley in California, to which they answered that they would not leave South Florida. The representatives from Google got up to leave immediately and while they were going out the door, told these guys that they ought to think about it overnight. The next day before they could even respond, an article came out in the paper announcing that Google had bought their competitor. No more thinking about it. Done and over that quick. Everyone knows Google is big and calls the shots. When they come to you, they are sure about you. But if you're not sure you want them, well, it's just not a good fit. They aren't giving you time to think about it. They don't need you because they're Google and there are so many others out there that want to be part of that.

To wrap it up, let's talk about a couple of important tips for building good solid relationships.

Express Gratitude and Appreciation

Gratitude is so important. You cannot say thank you enough. It is not always about the big things. It's about the little things like thanking someone for his or her time. Acknowledgethat someone's time is valuable. It doesn't matter if it's your client or the person who answers your phone. Their time is valuable to them, and you. Be gracious about the time someone is giving you. Whether it's your employee, a supplier or a client, they are taking time away from their purpose and giving it to you.

Always, always recognize people's value. People want to be appreciated. Dale Carnegie said: "The deepest urge in human nature is the desire to be important.… Always make the other person feel important." When I end a conversation, I always tell people that I appreciate them. I want them to feel like no one is more important than them in that moment.

Referrals

I'm always developing business, whether for myself or my clients. As I was checking out of the hotel during a business trip to Dallas, I made an inquiry as to the operating company for the hotel. I did this with the thought that perhaps H&H or another one of my clients might pick up some business there. One of the ways that I can help my clients is by uncovering opportunities to help them grow their business. They know I'm looking out for them and that increases my value in their eyes.

Questions

Who are your best clients?

_____

_____

_____

_____

What kind of relationship do you have with them now?

_____

_____

_____

_____

How can you duplicate that experience to all of your future clients?

_____

_____

_____

_____

_____

How often do you take the time show your appreciation to others?

_____

_____

_____

_____

In what ways do you help your clients grow?

_____

_____

_____

_____

_____

"Make the other person feel important – and do it sincerely."

Dale Carnegie

Chapter 6

You Get What You Ask For

I'm a firm believer in the mindset that you don't get what you don't ask for. It's really hard to do and do effectively. Perhaps that is why I embrace it. I know most of us freeze up when we have to ask for what we want, particularly if we are asking for money or help. I know something happens to me when I have to ask for either of those things. So how the heck are you going to get what you want if you don't ask for it?

Letting your prospective client know right out of the gate what your intentions are (also great communication tactic) sets the tone for doing business. It may be that you're seeking a long-term contract or a consult for improving your efficiency. It doesn't always have to be monetary. But you should always lead with what you want out of the relationship.

I needed to make money while I was going to college so I went to work in a restaurant. My first week there I spent making salads and sweeping the floor, the lowest of the low on the totem pole. One day the general manager came in and asked how I was doing and if he could do anything for me. I told him I was alright and didn't need anything. Then I blurted out that I just wanted to do more. I liked working and I was a hard worker. But I really didn't like making salads or sweeping floors (although I did both with a smile). So he asked me what I was thinking and I boldly told him I wanted his job. About a year and a half down the road, I had his job when he was promoted.

Whether you think it was the laws of attraction at work or because I just asked for what I wanted, I got it. We opened up the restaurant together and then he quickly moved on. He took a position with a larger restaurant group in North Carolina and I moved up into his position.

Be clear about what you want. People aren't mind readers. Although I'm sure there are some that would like to be. They don't know what to give you unless you ask. No one is going to be able to just get what you want. Spell it out in black and white. And they're probably going to tell you what they want right back, hopefully. That's good. Then you can help them out. Conditions are set and that's when you start negotiating.

No for-profit business is in business for charity. Businesses are organized to make a profit and grow to realize more profit. Even nonprofits need to make a profit. Not being afraid to present yourself and ask clearly for what you want simplifies your life and your counterpart's life. They can either satisfy your needs, or not. If not, you just break away before wasting anyone's time. The only thing better than a yes is a no, right? Sets the intentions straight up. You either get down to business or move on. It's that simple.

Uncertainty (risk) kills businesses. You never want a maybe answer. It's wishy-washy and leaves too many things open for interpretation. You saw how Google operates in the last chapter. Google heard the firm down in South Florida say it didn't want to play if it had to move its operation. It left them with what they thought was a chance to re-think their offer, then promptly moved on to hire their competitor. When you get to the table, you must have your skin in the game. You must be clear about what you want you may miss out.

Curveball: I like to paint murals. I'm not great at it but it's something I do and something I love. For most amateur muralists, asking for what you want is not easy. It's a skill. It's a skill that needs to be developed. You have to practice it regularly. I use my painting hobby to practice all the time. I go into businesses to see if they might want a mural painted on their wall. It's a way for me to practice my cold calls. Because that's what it is. Except that, for me, the value is that I get to paint whatever I want. I get to refine my painting skills, something I'm new at, doing something that enriches my lifestyle.

The doubt that comes with having to ask for what you want is a self-imposed psychological barrier. I believe it has a great deal to do with your self-esteem and past experiences. It's listening to the negative voice in your head telling you that that it's a stupid idea or it's too early or you're being too aggressive. The fact is, it might be too early or aggressive. But you can still move forward if you do it the right way. If you know who you're talking to and say it the right way, you can set up that foundation for the deep relationship I spoke about before.

Don't get me wrong. You aren't going to just come out and say, "Here's my price. My product/service will help you." First you need to understand the pain point, or problem, so you leverage your solution. If you learn what a specific pain point is and your solution doesn't fit, that's when you start to negotiate. You ask them what needs to happen in order for them to give you what you want, their business. It's a back-and-forth exchange of wants, collaborations and solutions.

In the beginning, I was horrible, just horrible, at asking for what I wanted. I had to practice, practice, practice. When I first started making phone calls, I would stutter on the phone. I would write out what I was supposed to say and still couldn't effectively read it. I was so nervous on the phone, you could hear it on the other end of the line.

It was so bad that one day my CEO took me out to lunch and said, "Trace, man, you've gotta relax." He's Southern Baptist and doesn't drink a drop, but joked that a drink might help calm my nerves. Of course, that wasn't advice but just shows you how nervous I was. But here's what you do. You take yourself out of the equation. Remind yourself it's about the business and something larger than yourself. It's the product and about how it's going to solve the problem for the person on the other end of the phone line. It's about knowing who you're talking to on a deeper level.

So why are people so afraid? It's about rejection. We all have a fear of being rejected. No one likes rejection. There is another component and that is confidence. I've been in sales pretty much since I started my first business. When people approached me, I didn't have any problem selling. But when I had to go out and get the business, that changed everything. Suddenly I had no confidence. I was filled with self-doubt. My negative voice jumped up in my face and started questioning everything I was doing. Darn! How did this suddenly get to be so hard?

When you go out to buy something, you're in control and have confidence when you're standing in front of that sales guy. You know what you want, and you know what you're willing to pay for the offering. Now turn the tables and imagine you're the sales guy. You sell yourself. If you could just project that confidence you have when you are buying or marketing something, people would eat it up. People need what you have to offer, right?

People eat up passion. It's contagious and your audience thrives on it. When you are mastering the art of the ask, remember that passion sells. People can see that you are not asking in a selfish way. It's that passion that people crave and makes them want what you have. I've seen dispassionate people try to sell something and it's a big turn-off. Your consumers aren't going to get excited about something you aren't excited about because it's not believable. If you're not confident in your ask, the underlying message you are communicating is that you're not confident in your product or service.

Think about telemarketers. You're probably already in a negative place when that phone rings and you know there's going to be someone trying to sell you something on the other end. If you pick up the phone and hear this timid voice, you're either in their face or just hanging up the phone. But if you pick up that phone and hear excitement and passion in the voice on the other end, you might listen to what they have to say (at least for a few seconds longer, which is sometimes all they need to make the close). It works; it must because it's a multibillion-dollar industry. In fact, **IBIS**World forecasts the

U.S. telemarketing industry to reach $28 billion in 2019 That's a lot of bucks.

How many times have you gone to a restaurant and you can tell the server is just doing a job to get by? I call these people order takers because that's all they really do. They don't get me excited about the food or atmosphere and they don't inspire me to come back. Other times you get a cracker-jack waiter or waitress who is clearly passionate about the restaurant and menu. The passion and the way that feeling is communicated get you excited about the food. The server makes you feel like you can trust his or her pallet. He or she makes you feel important. They have passion and it's infectious.

Let your personality shine! Have you ever gone through a drive-through and the person on the speaker is all bubbly and when he or she asks what you want gets just totally excited about your answer? Before you know it, you've supersized your meal and ordered extra because he or she is so happy and cheerful. You don't even want to tell the person no because he or she is so cute! Well, that is personality plus and it sells. Use your personality. People love it. When you shine, they want to shine right back. You make their day better because you made them smile.

Some time back, I met my now-girlfriend for the first time. We did the usual and met at a cocktail spot in a vibrant part of Denver. We hit it off pretty well and decided to go out to dinner. So I flexed a bit to impress her and made a call to a very popular restaurant to see if I could get us in. I knew the wait was going to be about an hour, but I wanted to impress. I had cultivated a pretty good relationship with the manager back when the restaurant first opened and took a lot of clients there, so I was pretty confident we would get a table. I made the call. When I spoke to the reservationist, she wasn't too accommodating. I tried to talk her into it but without success. That's when I asked to speak to the manager I knew. She came on the line and I explained what I wanted. She told me she would make an exception for me this time, but she could not guarantee that she would do it next time. Here's the point:1) I asked for what I wanted. And I got it. 2) The manager agreed but established boundaries and set the expectation that it was not a given it would happen again.

Don't be afraid to ask for what you want. Asking is the most important part of establishing ground rules and understanding everyone's expectations from the start. One thing I know for absolute certain is if you don't ask, there is no possibility of getting what you want.

Questions

Are you afraid of the ask? Why?

_____

_____

_____

_____

List three positive experiences you've had with a sales person?

_____

_____

_____

_____

What did they do that made the experience positive/memorable?

_____

_____

_____

_____

What can you do to practice asking and build your confidence?

_____

_____

_____

_____

"Those who can ask without shame are viewing themselves in collaboration with – rather than in competition with – the world."

Amanda Palmer

Chapter 7

Ask for Help

This chapter is about asking for what you need. There is a difference between want and need. Need is about asking for help. Whether it's asking a family member, a manager or CFO, business partner or just someone you're working with for help. When there is a moment of uncertainty or you are facing an unknown, rather than learning a lesson the hard way, you never fear asking for ask for the help you need when you need it.

Why is it so difficult for us to ask for help? Humans seem to be inherently afraid of asking for help. I have no doubt that those of you who are reading this right now have had one or more experiences where you knew you needed help but didn't ask for it and in hindsight realized your situation would have been so much easier if you had just asked for the help you needed at the time.

When I was deep into my pin manufacturing business, I got rid of the retail and wholesale sectors of my business so that I could direct my focus solely toward the manufacturing side. I had this one client that made road signs that said, "This Is A Good Sign." He created them for open-minded people to let them know they were in the right place at the right time. A symbol of positivity. The signs reminded them that they were staying on the right track.

So, one day owner came to me and asked if he could go on payment terms. Honestly, that had me scratching my head because I didn't have any idea about payment terms or how to extend credit to my client. I didn't know the first step of setting someone up on terms. I didn't know what the legalities were, how to set up a contract or even the first thing about how to implement terms. But I thought about it a bit and decided to take a risk. I told him he could pay me in 30 days. It was a big risk, too, because I didn't even ask the guy for anything in writing. Well, you guessed it. He didn't pay me in 30 days. He didn't pay me until five years later and not what he owed me.

I learned a huge lesson from that experience, one of the best lessons I ever learned: What I had failed to do was to ask for help. I didn't even go to my father, who is in the factoring business. Our own family business had the answers. Man, this guy must have seen me coming a mile away. The thing is, I would not have had to go through the problems and aggravation created by this guy if I had only asked for help. But I didn't ask. Instead, I learned the hard way. I offered terms to a client with no credit and got burned. I made a completely uninformed decision.

Most psychologists will tell you that the No. 1 reason people don't and won't ask for help is fear. Fear that others will perceive us as being weak or incompetent probably tops the list. We have this illogical mentality that others might think you're not strong enough to handle things on your own if we ask for help. Perhaps there is also the vulnerability that we will know that we don't know something. Then there is the simple and very common fear of rejection. If we ask for help and someone tells us no, many of us get crushed. We live in a culture that fosters the idea that we must be strong and know everything –"I don't need help from anyone, I got this!"

Payment Terms: Payment terms are conditions set for the seller to complete the sale. The terms specify the time allowed for a buyer to pay off the amount due. For instance, if you've ever had remodeling done on your house, the contractor may have set up terms where you paid a third of the cost up front, a third of the cost half-way through the job and the final third when the job was complete.

There are so many reasons why we don't ask for help. Yet there are also very important truths about why we should positively be asking for help when we need it. Overcoming your fear of weakness or rejection shows strength. Asking for help is more a sign of strength than a weakness. People who don't ask for help when they need it are at risk for making big mistakes that can be very costly. Sometimes the business does not recover from those mistakes, either.

People genuinely want to help entrepreneurs and business owners. People will jump at the chance to help you. They'll share their knowledge and experiences with you ad nauseam. There is a sense of pride when you help a business owner overcome or prevent an obstacle. Everyone wants to be a hero. I am sure that if someone asked, you wouldn't hesitate to help.

Too often, our ego steps in and we end up learning the hard way. If only we could stop letting our ego get in the way and holding us back because we are so worried about how others perceive us. There is always someone out there who is willing to help us if we just ask. It doesn't matter what about. It doesn't need to be about payments terms. Maybe you have a problem employee. Maybe you are having an issue with a vendor. What if you have a different kind of problem with a client and you're not sure what to do?

Look up your local SCORE chapter (SCORE is a national nonprofit network of volunteer business mentors and a partner of the U.S. Small Business Administration), entrepreneur associations and small-business development center (these are also SBA partners). These types of organizations are a wealth of information there solely to help your business thrive. The tax dollars you generate as a business owner are very valuable to your municipality so it's in their best interest that you succeed.

I am dealing with a client in the construction industry that had just learned about factoring and came to us for help. Most factoring companies won't play in the construction industry because it's very high-risk, which is why I needed to collect all the extra information up front.

This company has taken out loan upon loan upon loan just to purchase materials and make payroll. It's trying desperately to keep the business afloat because of cash-flow issues. Now that it knows about factoring, it's looking for this service to be its safety net. As I said, most factoring companies won't even play in construction, but we decided the risk might be worth it. After all, the deal could result in Dorado realizing $150,000 annually. However, we also didn't want to lose well over half of a million dollars making mistakes and learning about how to operate in this volatile niche.

What did I do next? I reached out to some of our competitors, people who know and respect our business and my father. People who've been in our industry a while and who have had some experience doing business with construction companies. I wanted to find out all they knew. I was on a call with a colleague for more than an hour. He shared every piece of information he had on dealing with construction companies, things to watch out for that could trip you up. Some were obvious and some not so obvious. Those that were not so obvious could have been very costly. In some cases, it could just come down to a single word in the master service agreement that could change the whole meaning of the contract.

There is also a fine line between knowing what your customer needs and what your advisors tell you. You need to be careful and not just take every piece of information given to you as an absolute. I was watching an interview with Jeff Bezos, founder, chairman, CEO and president of Amazon, and he was talking about going against the status quo. Basically, he said that when you go against the status quo, you're going to have a lot of people that might try to steer you in a different direction. He gave an example of Amazon Web Services (AWS). He believes if he had gone to his advisors

---

Amazon Web Services (AWS) is a cloud-based service that offers Operating Services, Security, Networking, Storage, Business Intelligence, Databases, Developer Options, and Machine Learning and other similar services.

---

about doing web services, they would have unanimously advised against it. Why? Because their opinions were that Amazon was a logistics company and web services were not in its wheelhouse. Now AWS is critical to amazon's development in all areas of the business.

My point is that most factoring companies don't deal with construction companies because of the risks, therefore, at Dorado Finance, we are going against the status quo by taking them on. We've looked at it and feel it's in our interest and worthwhile for us to at least investigate the possibilities. So we're reaching out to people that are experts or have experience in this area that can best advise us on the pros and cons of this type of client base. But we also know that we need to carefully weigh all the facts and information given to us before we decide whether we are willing to take the risk.

There are people like us out there that can help you. I'm in the factoring business. If you need help bringing in your accounts receivable, my company can help you do that. We can free you up so that you can focus on the important things like running and growing your business. We can save you from the costly mistake of taking out loans to meet your payroll and continue operations. If we can't help you, there are people out there like us that may be able to help you in other ways. And we are glad to point you in their direction.

Nobody wants to leave someone hanging. Don't let your ego take over and interfere with reaching out for help. Ask for what you need. It's such a simple concept, yet so hard for so many of us. It's really a sign of respect for the person you are asking to help you. You are paying tribute to his or her expertise when you go to them. It tells them that you respect them enough request their expertise.

When you surround yourself with people with whom you have built deep and lasting relationships, you have many resources that can help you. Situations you come across are never going to be exactly the same. There is no way to anticipate *everything* that life throws at you. You can try to anticipate things that may happen, except the thing that actually happens won't be what you expected. And when you try to anticipate that thing happening in the future, something different will inevitably come at you. Having a pool of resources to help you is paramount. It can save you from having to go through some very hard learning experiences. It can ultimately save you from making serious and pricey mistakes; mistakes that could even cost you your business. Asking for help is a critical component of success.

Questions

Are you in a situation right now where you need help?

_____

_____

_____

What do you need help with?

_____

_____

_____

Who can you go to that may have been in a similar situation?

_____

_____

_____

_____

Is factoring an option for managing your invoices so you can focus on operations and growing your business?

_____

_____

_____

_____

"Whether we're talking about leadership, teamwork, or client service, there is no more powerful attribute than the ability to be genuinely honest about one's weaknesses, mistakes, and needs for help."

Patrick Lencioni

Chapter 8

Be Creative

The No. 1 reason for people to use factoring is growth. If you're coming to me for factoring, it tells me that you are 100 percent successful. If a company is selling us its invoice, it tells me it needs that money to go out and get another client. It is flipping the money just like we are. We're flipping it on invoices, they're flipping it on people or infrastructure or something else to grow their business.

You don't have to constantly re-invent the wheel. But when an obstacle presents itself, get creative. You know there's the status quo, the traditional way of doing things. Some people might even take an obstacle and decide not to go through it or around it. This is where they stop. They just don't feel it's worth it to them to deal with it. Then there's the creative way of dealing with things.

Look at the situation. Take some time to reflect on it and understand where the obstacle came from and why it came to be. Try to figure out why it wasn't predicted already. Get creative with it. Assess the situation and look at the facts and the value. What's malleable?

To be successful in any business, you need to listen to your instincts and be able to bend and flex when necessary. You need to think of doing things in ways maybe nobody else has thought of before. Bending and flexing allows you to be creative. It's what you do to solve problems, right? Problem-solvers are naturally creative. They can weather the obstacles that present themselves unexpectedly because they are flexible and know when to bend.

Whether it's finding money through factoring or trying out a new idea on social media, staying creative and not marooning yourself on your own island is essential to advancing and profiting from your business. Maybe the first thing you tried didn't work. Maybe even the second thing you tried wasn't successful. So you keep adjusting and tweaking things until they do work. I am always re-evaluating things and making small tweaks here and there to improve my processes, relationships, products and everything we do in our business. That's what keeps it fresh and moving forward.

Todd Duncan and his wife Deb Duncan wrote a New York Times bestseller, "The $6,000 Egg, The 10 New Golden Rules of Customer Service." In it, there is a story about a couple who went to the same restaurant on a regular basis, maybe twice a week. Those are the best patrons to have if you're in the restaurant business. The gist of the story is that the man wanted an egg on his burger, which was not a normal item on the menu. The server asked the kitchen if it was possible to add the egg to the man's burger, and was told no. The man knew the eggs cost about 50 cents each but was willing to pay an extra $2 for the addition of the egg. But the manager refused, explaining that the eggs were for the breakfast menu and he could not take one of the eggs from the breakfast inventory and add it to the man's burger. It just wasn't done. Of course, this upset the man. So he and his wife left the restaurant without buying a meal, walked to a nearby market that cooked fresh food to order and had an egg added to their pizza. They never returned to the restaurant again.

That small decision by the manager not to waver and stay steadfast cost the restaurant $6,000 that day, hence the title of the book, "The $6,000 Egg." How hard would it have been for the manager to accommodate his customer? Wouldn't you think he could have sold a single egg to make his long-time and valuable customer happy? It would have taken very little effort. The man was even willing to pay substantially more for the upgrade to his burger. It may have even turned into an unexpected boost in future revenue. Think about it. They could have added a burger with a fried egg to their specialty menu and charged more for it. And who knows, it may have become a standard menu item for the restaurant in the future.

The kind of rigid inflexibility displayed by this manager cost his restaurant in more ways than one. Not only did they lose valuable customers, but the couple would surely have been compelled to tell their story to their friends. And their friends would probably think twice about going to that restaurant. Word of mouth can be your greatest asset or your worst nightmare.

Being rigid, failing to adapt and refusing to accommodate your customers will kill your business. Businesses that are willing to bend and flex to solve problems for their customers are going to be more successful. They're able to grow much faster by building better relationships with their customers. Customers remember when you are willing to help them out when they need it. It goes back to helping businesses stay in business. Maya Angelou said, "People will forget what you did, but people will never forget how you made them feel."

Getting referrals from your clients is the best form of advertising you have, and it's free. Word of mouth is the most valuable and effective asset a company can have. Testimonials, good or bad, have more impact on your business than any advertising billboard or something seen in a TV ad. Think about it. How many times do you make your decision to buy something, try a new restaurant or perhaps go to see a new movie based on online reviews? It's the very purpose of sites like Angie's List and Yelp. Consumers are going to look at those reviews before making their decision. That is word-of-mouth advertising at its best. And those testimonials will have a major impact on whether you get more business or people bypass you. It's all about your customers and your willingness to think outside the box when they come to you for a creative solution.

When I was in software, I was responsible for a virtual retinal disease diagnostic center that was under the medical direction of Johns Hopkins. I was responsible for 90-plus retina surgeons in 45 states. We would on-board new positions for the people who did the interpretations of the retinal images, looking at vascularization in the back of the eye for signs of diabetic complications and other issues. These doctors would come be working in their clinics at 7 a.m. and work until 8 p.m. It didn't matter what time zone they were in; we had to be there to cover for them. My day was based on the 9-to-5 model, but it was never a 9-to-5 day. I would frequently have training at 11 at night or 5 in the morning in order to cover all time zones and accommodate their shifts. That's how we made our business work.

These guys were a critical component of the department and especially to the patients they served. It was vital to these patients that the images were interpreted quickly and the results reported back to the primary care physicians quickly so the care loop could be closed. That was the level of service our clients expected and we provided.

This is where you develop those deep relationships. By being there for our customer across all time zones and at all hours of the day or night, we demonstrated their importance to us. We showed them that we understood their business, their client's importance to them and on a regular basis how much we valued them.

There are exceptions to the norm, though, when flexing and bending aren't going to work. Back when I was in the pin business, I had a client that wanted its pin orders processed really fast. It was an unrealistic turnaround time for me and no matter how flexible or creative I got, I was not going to be able to commit to their timeframe. I knew I had to let them go. I was going to have to refer them to a competitor that was a better fit for them. I knew they would get charged more, but sometimes that is the price of doing business. And it's not a bad thing. It meant they were growing. They were graduating to a new level and I wasn't their best partner anymore. I did them a service by letting them go, but it was a decision that also had the potential to help me down the line. That customer was going to remember that I had their best interests in mind, even it if meant discontinuing our partnership at the time. Down the road when my business graduated to a new level, I might have the opportunity to pick them up again. It all goes back to the value of those deep relationships you develop.

When you're first starting out and trying to grow your business, you will probably find that you have to bend and flex a lot. You'll need to be super creative sometimes in order to offer your clients the right solution to their problem. Hopefully you'll grow as you go and eventually graduate to new levels. You may find in growing your business that you've progressed to a point where you can't be as creative as you used to be for some clients. You may have to pick and choose from some of the great relationships you've built over the years. Or you may have a new client that maybe isn't a very good client. At these times you may have to make executive decisions that are hard, but in the best interest of your company, to let them go. There are times when you just have to make the tough choice in order stay in business and continue to grow.

At the end of the day, it's all about your customer and solving their problems. And sometimes, even your own. In order to do that, you have to be malleable. Be willing to stretch and get creative in order to solve their problems. Being nimble plays a huge part in building deep relationships and bonds with your clients that last. It's also about growth and maturing your own business besides.

Take this book for instance. I went to my publisher and told them I wanted to write a book about disruption. They told me up front that they didn't publish books like that. So I had to go back and get creative. I started thinking it through and asking myself some questions. I listed the facts as I knew them at the time:

1. I wanted to write a book.

2. I know the book is going to have a tremendous positive and valuable impact on what I want to accomplish, whatever that is.

3. How can I add value to someone's life through a guide?

It took a couple of months, a considerable amount of thinking and some driving around, but here I am, having written this book. Creativity, and especially timing, is crucial in anything you do. And that was the right time for me to step out of the box, get creative and write this book.

Questions

What phase are you in your business? Just starting out or graduating to new levels?

_____

_____

_____

_____

Does one or more of your clients have a unique problem that you don't typically respond to?

_____

_____

_____

_____

Is there an opportunity here for you to get creative and offer an out-of-the-box solution that would solve their problem?

_____

_____

_____

_____

What is your creative option? Write it down.

_____

_____

_____

_____

_____

_____

_____

_____

"If opportunity doesn't knock, build a door"

Milton Berle

Chapter 9

The Whale Philosophy

There are a couple of schools of thought related to your business. I've always liked what I'll call "the whale" philosophy. I prefer the larger clients, especially when putting it into perspective with our typical clients. These larger clients are relatively accessible when it comes to needing services. Once you've gone through all the lessons and exercises and you've reached the point where you can actually start calling on potential clients, there's a lot to be said for these large guys. Because if you can reel in and perform and fulfill your service for a whale, that is a monumental accomplishment, especially when you are growing your business. Think about all we talked about so far about developing relationships and using them to leverage your network, establishing what you want and asking for help when you need it. That help you're asking for could mean you need more business.

You go to your whale clients to get more business. These whales move slower. They just do. So, if you want to take them on, you need to offer them terms. They're going to pay you in 30-60 days no matter what. It doesn't matter if you give them terms on delivery, 15 or 30 days. They're going to pay when they are ready to pay. It's just how it works. That's what you're going to have to live with if you're going to engage in business with larger clients. Why? Because the longer they hold on to the cash, the more they can do with it. That's why having cash now is so valuable…you can use more of it for a longer duration.

But larger clients are going to be the ones that dramatically propel your business forward because they are the influencers. And influencers go out and do what they do: influence other influencers. They may be early adopters of your solution and give you the greatest insight on how to add even more value to your proposition.

This all kind of goes back to knowing your audience and being able to identify their needs and pain points. What solutions can you bring to the table that your competitors can't? Or have you been able to uncover some pain points they are experiencing with their current solution provider? Leverage your solution with these big companies. Show them you can provide a solution that stops the pain. You can offer a rebate or guarantee incentive that will give you the opportunity to earn their business.

So, what are these large customers seeking? There is an extraordinary strength of purpose when you are talking to a whale at a high level like the C-suite. These guys know and capture the essence of the entrepreneurial spirit. They understand you've worked your butt off just to get in front of them. They get the incredible persistence and tenacity it took for you to get to them, whether you're standing or sitting in front of them or on the phone with them. Just by getting in front of those people speaks volumes.

I learned from the whales that they can show a lot of loyalty. If you consistently deliver and honor your commitment to them, they will deliver for you. That isn't to say they are all good. Not everyone operates at the same level of integrity and I've got some stories in the factoring business to prove it.

We have $300,000 tied up with a publicly traded energy company and they're refusing to pay. They approved everything. We don't just buy invoices willy-nilly. They got back to us and had approved the billing. Suddenly, oil prices plummeted and lost 30 percent of their value. At that point, the company just decided to refuse to pay. That's the kind of scary thing about being in business with a whale. Don't get discouraged, though. There's always going to be one or two bad apples out there. That's just the law of percentages. But the majority of whales I've dealt with are reputable and good clients. And that offsets any less-than-desirable experiences I've had.

It goes back to what I was saying earlier about letting some clients go. When I was running my pin business, I basically got to a point where I stopped doing the small orders and just went after the larger business. I began to service restaurant franchises and high-value organizations like the Lion's Club. I picked up a secret aviation club made up of pilots and a pyramid-type organization out of Michigan that gave out award pins as members moved up the ranks. They only ordered about four or five times a year, but every order was for 1,000 or more pins. It saved me a lot of time and I had a much higher profit margin from producing the larger volumes. I was also able to provide a higher level of customer service because it was easier dealing with one client rather than managing bunches of issues spread out over a number of smaller clients.

When you first start out you need to rely on your network to help you generate revenue. When you're established as a legitimate business and have proven there is a need and demand for your product or services in the marketplace, that's when you can go after the whales. Whales are less sensitive to pricing. You can get bigger margins from whales or, if you don't get bigger margins, you have higher tickets.

My philosophy is that when you start out, don't go after the whales first. Prove yourself in the marketplace first. Once you've proven yourself, start going after the whales. There are many benefits to capturing a whale. They already have established value in the marketplace, which provides them with many options. They are the influencers of the marketplace they are in. You spend less time by dealing with one entity, enabling you execute your solution a higher level. And that frees you up to spend more time concentrating on growing your business to a new level.

One of the things you should fully understand about going after whales is if you are out there chasing whales, you need to know that you are in the rejection business. You're going to get told no so many times it will make your head hurt. Embrace the rejection, reflect on it and learn from it. Then take what you've learned when you go after your next whale. This is the epitome of being an entrepreneur. When someone tells you no, you have something to think about. Those rejections carry incredibly valuable lessons if you look at them the right way. They give you an opportunity to reflect and learn. It's a pivot point where you know you need to adjust and deliberate on what happened.

Ask yourself questions: Did I not communicate clearly? Did I ask the right questions? Did I offer the right value? There are so many things to look at, each filled with lessons to learn. Maybe it just isn't the right client for you. If so, why not?

Perhaps you don't have the right solution for this client. There are so many things that come into play. You're going to get rejected more often than not. But it's those rejections that give you the most to reflect on and ultimately equip you with the lessons and tools you need to be successful when you take on the next one.

Man, oh man, though, when you land that whale, that is a big and loud hallelujah. Your confidence soars and you are on a total sales high. Be careful, though, because that one success can be a double-edged sword. On the one hand, you've leveled up successfully. That's cause for celebration for sure. And you have demonstrated your position in the marketplace. You're where you feel you should be. You're closer to your vision. But there can be a dark side, too. Sometimes when we win big, we can get overly confident and that can be a reason for being rejected by the next whale.

It's important to recognize and celebrate your achievement. But don't get so overly confident and think that just because you got this one, you're automatically going to get the next. If you got one, you got only one. It doesn't mean that you're undoubtedly going to get No. 2 or 3 or 4. Because they are whales and they are bigger than you.

Be sure that you know who the true whales are. There are a lot of companies out there that can look like they're a whale, but it's a charade. In reality, they have major cash-flow issues and other problems. Look at casinos. They appear to be whales and have a lot of cash, but they don't. So the cover doesn't always reveal what's inside. This is where you have to make sure you conduct your due diligence. Look at the health of the business. Look at the longevity of the leadership. Drill down deep into the finances and the industry they are in or support. Understand if the industry is healthy and what it looks like for the future.

Norway is one of only two nations globally that officially practices commercial whaling, the other being Iceland. Norway officially objected to the 1986 international moratorium that was placed on commercial whaling. And the country still does not respect it.

Here is a perfect example. This has to do with what went down in Iceland in early 2019. Iceland decided to ignore the international whaling ban of 1986 and issued licenses to allow for the killing of 2,000 whales between 2019 and 2025. It's questionable why the fishermen would want to do this. Iceland's whale-watching tourism business has exploded, contributing revenues of almost double those of the whale hunters. But for some reason, these guys decided to still go out and harvest whales. One wonders why they would make that kind of decision because if you look at the industry, the money is in the eco-tourism and no longer in hunting and harvesting the meat.

It sounds like a bad pun talking about real whales and whales as a large client. The thing is, it's a real-life example of making sure you fully understand whether the whale you are going after is a true whale or just a charade. Iceland's whale meat market may look like it's a good opportunity on the outside, but if you delved into it deeper, you would see that the whale tourism, not the whale meat market, is the real opportunity.

My philosophy is to go after the whale. Capture the big guy. Remember that whales have many options. They are the influencers of the marketplace they are in. You will spend less time dealing with one person, which means you can deliver a higher level of service. It frees up more of your time so you can concentrate on growing your business to a new level. But be careful. Some companies and industries that appear to be whales may not be. Be thorough and do your due diligence. Celebrate your wins but don't allow yourself to get cocky and think you're going to win every time.

Questions

List two or three whales you would like to go after right now.

_____

_____

_____

_____

What kind of company are they? What do you know about them so far?

_____

_____

_____

_____

What do you need to learn about them and their industry?

_____

_____

_____

_____

Have you previously gone after a whale and been rejected?
What did you learn?

_____

_____

_____

_____

"A satisfied customer is the best business strategy of all."

Michael Leboeuf

Chapter 10

Leveraging Your Assets

Factoring is a way to fulfill payment terms and act as a collection agency for the invoices you send to your customers. As you're growing, you've got multiple obligations – employees, equipment, operating expenses, etc. You need to have cash in hand to be able to meet your obligations. Waiting 30, 60 or 90 days to get it is not an option. You don't want to take out loans so you can meet your payroll or operational expenses. If you do that, you'll soon find yourself in way over your head and a debt that is so big you'll may never be able to dig yourself out.

Leveraging your assets by selling your invoices to a factoring company will get you the cash you need to move your business forward. It's like having built-in equity. Let's assume I decide to start a trucking company. It takes very little to do this. All you need is a truck and a cell phone. From there you can arrange with a client to pick up a load and drop it off at an appointed place and time. After you've completed the job, you send the client an invoice. Great! But now you've just used up all your cash. No cash and you still have to gas up your truck and wash it before your next job. Obviously, you're going to need more cash, and you need it today. You can't wait for the 30 days it typically takes to get paid on your invoice.

If you were to use a factoring company, you could get the money for that invoice up front. Now you have cash in hand you can use to buy gas and wash your truck. You might even be able to set some money aside that you can use to lease a fleet of trucks. Before you know it, you've saved enough to buy another truck and add a driver. It's basically about leveraging your assets over and over. It's a game of cash in and cash out so you can keep your business fueled while it grows.

When we advance cash to our clients, we have our own due diligence process. We look at each situation individually. We look at any other assets and how they can be leveraged to grow their business so you become more financially secure and stable in your day-to-day operations. We look at the assets and accounts receivables. We review all the possible risks. Then we get creative, which is now about protecting our business. It's not just about leveraging your assets. It's also about protecting our company on the back end. Look, if we don't protect ourselves, who's going to? Protecting yourself is a huge component in business. Because if you don't protect yourself and practice some form of some risk mitigation, you will end up learning a very hard lesson. I know this from personal experience.

A Uniform Commercial Code (UCC) filing is a type of lien. It's a notice that a lender has a security interest in one or more of your assets. The term comes from a collection of established rules that govern how commercial transactions work in the U.S.

Here are some of the things you can do to help protect your business when you are intending to take on a new client. Running a credit check on your prospective client is essential. File Uniform Commercial Code, or UCC, documents so that if the entity goes belly up, you've got a place in line for hopefully some of their debt paid back. UCCs are a type of collateral. It means that when money is owed and money is paid, you will be able to have some leverage in court.

Make sure you have the right things in place to protect yourself. You need to be very organized and diligent in your record-keeping. Assets can become valueless without the proper documentation. It doesn't happen often, but there are times you may have to go back into your records for some type of information such as a name, a check number, an address. You absolutely must be very meticulous in your record-keeping and communications so that if things come up, you can defend your right to get paid for your efforts. There are times when you will have to fight to get paid and if you don't have good records, you will have lost the battle before you started.

It doesn't even have to be a malicious act to end up in a court. It could have been an inadvertent misstep on the part of your client. Let's say I invoiced a large hotel chain for 56 hours of banquet services. For the sake of simplicity, we'll say the invoice was for $100,000. I send the hotel an invoice and in 45 days I received a check from them. But it was only written for $75,000. So, I call up the hotel chain and they agree that the invoice I sent was for 56 hours and $100,000. Then they tell me that according to their vendor management system, the other $25,000 probably didn't have a proper signature or maybe it was missing an item number and that's why it wasn't paid. It could have been any number of things, but let's just say that we found out the $25,000 was attributable to one person that didn't clock out of the hotel's vendor system every day. I had also kept a record of the caterer's time, so was able to show the hotel that my invoice was legitimate and accurate. The employee didn't have to clock out because we had kept a dual record of all the people employed by the caterer on this job. This is just one small example showing why it's so important that you keep meticulous records.

Leveraging your assets by hiring a factoring company to manage your invoices is a good way to make sure you always have cash in hand to meet your commitments to your clients and your employees, manage your operations and grow your business. Protect your assets. Make sure you also protect your business when you take on a new customer. Run credit checks, background checks, etc. Its worth the money upfront rather than a big loss on the backside. Keep complete documentation and accurate records to ensure you will get paid even if they go belly up.

Questions

What is your turnaround time on you accounts receivable?

_____

_____

_____

_____

Are you struggling to keep good cashflow?

_____

_____

_____

_____

Have you ever worked with a factoring company?

_____

_____

Would it be a viable option for you moving forward?

_____

_____

"Rule No. 1: Never lose money. Rule No. 2: Never forget Rule No. 1."

Warren Buffett

Chapter 11

Re-investing Is The Best Investing

By leveraging asset-based financing, your liquidity can quickly increase because of your consistent and immediate influx of cash. If you are a temp agency or dispatch company for example, you can take on larger jobs because you know that your only cost is to take on more workers.

I pulled the trigger on a lead-generating site because I noticed that one of our competitors had listed itself on a website as one of the best factoring companies in the country. And I just knew in my gut they were generating leads from this website. So I pulled the trigger on going with this site to see what would happen. Shortly thereafter, I received my first lead for a temp agency and I signed the contract within hours of receiving the lead.

The temp agency industry doesn't realize it yet, but it needs the factoring business as much as the trucking industry. The staffing agencies that we already service like H&H have achieved triple digit growth for the last three years. Some have grown their businesses into the millions because we free them from having to wait for invoice payments to come in.

Through my conversations with our clients that run staffing agencies, I've discovered that their success is based on the numbers of people they find that are willing to do the low-end jobs. It seems to be their only limitation. The only cost they incur is when an employee is hired out for a job. So it's a really agreeable business to be in. And we play an essential role in the success of their business. Our clients have to pay their employees on time, usually weekly. They can't wait for invoices to be paid 30, 45 or 60 days later. That's where we come in. We provide them with the cash they need up front. Because of us, they are able to meet their commitments to their clients and their employees as well as expand and grow their business.

I talk about H&H, one of our best staffing agency clients, often and how they've grown into a multimillion-dollar company in a matter of a couple years. Their greatest need in continuing to grow is to be able to supply more laborers. They cater to immigrants that come to the United States legally looking for a better life, usually for their children's' future. Their employees are the kind of people who are willing to do anything just to have a job and the privilege of living in the U.S. So they established their business in their own community. H&H is significant contributor in its community and its team is seen as leaders. People are attracted to them and their company. Many will just stop in to see what they are about or how they are doing, as if it is a social affair. Some of the people that were once employed by them still stop in to say hello even though they have been able to move on to more stable jobs. It's an incredible thing to witness and be a part of.

Their greatest need in growing is getting people and having the cash in hand to immediately pay them. The service that we provide allows them to keep everybody happy and their business sustainable. They have a reputation for being reliable. Word of mouth spreads quickly among their community, and that word-of-mouth advertising brings them more people and more clients. They are known for paying people right away. They hire quickly and their people are reliable. Everybody wins when they sign on with H&H. It's a virtuous circle in the truest sense.

They are invoicing as rapidly as they can, and we are processing their invoices as rapidly as we can. This gives them the confidence to continue growing. They rely on what you might say is an alternative bank. As a factoring company, we are able to provide them with the assurance that their assets are in good hands. That's important because they still have some liability with us. At the end of the day they are responsible for paying us back if their customer doesn't pay. But knowing we're there to make the collection calls it takes to get that money and stay on top of it even when their client is past the 30 days is valuable to them. It gives them peace of mind knowing there is someone fighting for them. Like the situation from the hotel chain where there was an error in payment, we were able to get the issue resolved for them quickly. It's great to have a factoring company when things are going well, but even more so when you need the clout of a bigger company to fight for you.

If you're in business now or thinking of getting into business, look into factoring as an option for handling your invoices. It could be the answer you need to get you off in hyper-growth mode quickly by keeping the cash in your hands. When you come to us, we also look at your whole business. We're not just looking at the accounts receivable. We're asking questions about your pain points, for sure, but we are also evaluating other things. Sometimes we uncover things you didn't even know you were struggling with. We are in business to give you peace of mind so that you can focus on the important task of operating and growing your business.

If your only limitation is money, if you're finding yourself fighting to make your bills at the end of the month, maybe you're just going through a rough time. It happens. Look into factoring. Whether it's my company or another, a factoring company can help you.

Questions

Are you struggling right now?

_____

_____

_____

_____

Are you worried that you're going to get paid?

_____

_____

_____

Are there things that are keeping you up at night?

_____

_____

_____

_____

Are you fighting to pay bills at the end of the month?

_____

_____

_____

_____

Ask yourself: Is factoring a viable option?

_____

_____

_____

_____

"Liquidity is a good proxy for relative net worth. You can't lie about cash, stocks, and bonds."

Mark Cuban

Chapter 12

Get Your Foot in The Door

You ask your clients if they know anyone else that would benefit from your solution. If your client benefited, then they probably know someone else that you think would benefit, as well. Ask them for a referral. That's how you really generate sales and strong clients. That's developing your business. It's getting to the heart of your business.

When I come across someone that's using another company for factoring, I start asking them questions. Nothing super-secret. They are not questions that would compromise their loyalty to their factor. I ask questions like, "How did you find out about them?" or "What do you like most about them?" "If they could do anything different that would make your life better, what would it be?" Everyone's got an opinion. Most are willing to share it. Once you know strengths and weaknesses you can take that with you to another whale you're trying to land. It could be as small as a person answering the phone live versus just having an automated menu gauntlet you have to go through to get to someone. There are many little things that add up. We're set up to exploit this.

You want to pick the low-hanging fruit. In the past when I first started working for that software startup, we were pre-revenue and it actually cost me money to get on board with them. So I created an alias to find out how our competitors did business. It gave us a good view into what they were doing versus what we were doing. It was all done organically. It gave us a lot of information we could act on. One example was the way they wrote their contracts. Did they bundle their solution options? Did the competitor sell each solution ala carte? Were they even able to provide all of the services? We researched their hardware and compared it to our hardware. We were able to capture two pictures within 60 seconds whereas most of the other hardware our competitors were using required some manual operation and there was a low first-capture time. We could speak to our customers about our strengths that bested our competitors. That highlighted their weakness.

Knowing what your competitor is doing gives you a strategic advantage. I learned that one of our competitors had submitted an algorithm to the Food and Drug Administration and was awaiting approval. I just called the number listed on google and spoke to the person that answered the phone to learn most of the information I wanted to know. We chose not to submit our algorithm because we knew that if we waited, we could just potentially take advantage of the precedent they set (and pay for). We already had the algorithm. We just didn't want to spend the millions of dollars it would take to get it approved by the FDA. So in that way, we exploited our competitor by allowing them to go through the painful and expensive process of getting approvals and then swooping in afterward. It's not unethical. They knew as much about us as we know about them. And they are going to use the things they know about me just as hard to gain the advantage they need.

Play the game as if others are also doing everything in their power to take away the business from you. As a growing business. you should always be asking what you're doing right and how you can do it even better. Look for your own weaknesses by understanding what your competitors are doing so you can fix them before your competitors use them to their advantage. Every business has weakness, some more than others. It's about finding those weaknesses and using them to set you apart from your competitor and win the business.

Even the big whales have weaknesses. Their speed of customer service is slow. Maybe when you call them for service, you have to go through a major phone gauntlet to get to someone who can help you. And then when you finally get through, you find out they can't help you and transfer you to someone else. But Dorado is personable and accessible so our culture is to answer the phone right away without the use of an auto-teller. That gives Dorado an advantage because people want that personal service that Dorado provides. I know this because I hear people complain about automated answering services all the time. Think about it yourself!

Have you ever called into a big company for service and get transferred around about five times before you get to someone who might be able to help you? Or my favorite, the various levels of service starting with the low-end guy and ultimately ending up with the specialist who won't get back to you for 48 hours. It happens all the time. Again, we have the advantage of being on the line right when you call.

This could be the culture of your company if it serves your vision. You keep it even if it's a bit of an expense. When you have that kind of advantage, you make it part of your DNA and you hold onto it for life. It's what is going to set you apart and that service will be what sets you apart because everybody has a product that can do the job. Might not do it as well, but it still does it. The one thing that will give you the best advantage is the how you execute the solution you provide. I think if you look at your own personal experiences, you would agree that you are most likely to be in favor of a company that provides a good product, but even better, excellent customer service.

Questions

Who are your competitors?

_____

_____

_____

Do you know their weaknesses?

_____

_____

_____

_____

What are they?

_____

_____

_____

_____

If you compare apples to apples, how do you compare?

_____

_____

_____

_____

What are your weaknesses? How can you improve?

_____

_____

_____

_____

"The ultimate competitive advantage is being cognitive."

Ginni Rometty

Chapter 13

Know Your Client Persona

We've talked about targeting your audience. In this chapter we're going to talk about knowing and understanding your client's persona, character. Who are they? What are their values? Every company develops a unique culture based on values. These values define the individual and collective behavior of how a company conducts itself. Think of your persona as your personal brand. It's how you present yourself to the world. When I meet a potential client for the first time, I am assessing not only their financial portfolio, but also painting a visual picture of them that tells me who they are, the kinds of decisions they make, the intangibles that are important to them, etc.

As a small factoring firm, we know our clients' journeys. We understand the risks they've taken to build a business of their own. We are also in the business of risk, so we identify with the struggles they face every day just to stay alive and grow. We have walked in their shoes and we know their battle scars. Whether you are coming to us or we are coming to you, we know we can help. It's different for a bank. Banks They tend to be large and operate within a more corporate-based culture. The humanness of your business is set aside in favor of reduced risk.

Our business is family owned. You might say I was born into it. Someone recently asked me if I would describe the culture of our company. I answered easily. It's *la familia*. Our employees and clients are family. Our employees now are the same women I grew up seeing and knowing at the office until I was out on my own. That's how long many of them have been with us. It's why we understand our clients so well. We have the very similar values as they do. We operate with integrity and conduct our business honestly. And we have built deep relationships and bonds with our clients, so much so that they often drop by the office and even bring their kids. That's because many are also family-owned businesses. In fact, 90 percent of our clients are family owned businesses. Our purpose is to help these families survive and grow and thrive. We're not in this business to make money, although we're certainly not in business to lose money. We feed our family, and we feed six other families. Our business exists to support families.

Look at the persona of potential clients. Visualize them and look for the same aspects of their persona that you see in yourself. Get to know their culture and understand the journey they have taken to get here. In this way, you will be able to empathize with their struggles and sacrifices. You can ask better questions to uncover their pain points. And understand their wants and needs. Then you can build a good partnership and create those deep relationships.

Questions

Describe your company's persona.

_____

_____

_____

_____

Now describe the persona of your typical client.

_____

_____

_____

_____

Do you have similar cultural values?

_____

_____

Do you know and understand their journey?

_____

_____

_____

_____

How does knowing these things help you to be a better business partner?

_____

_____

_____

_____

"Surround yourself with people that reflect who you want to be and how you want to feel, energies are contagious."

Rachel Wolchin

Chapter 14

Cash Is King

There's a saying: A dollar today is worth more than a dollar tomorrow. Think about how often you've seen the price of a product or service you know of that has gone down. Something always goes up. Rarely do prices go down. So it's easy to deduce that your money is going buy you more today than it will tomorrow. Maybe it's upgrading to more user-friendly software or acquiring another type of asset. It could be anything. By using a factoring service, you will be able to leverage your cash to get the best value out of it today.

You've got to think about it in terms of your business. If you have cash today, you can do more for your business right now. It not only lets you to operate in the best interest of your own business but also allows your clients to better serve their customers. Because that's why they are in business, right? Your customers are there to serve its customers. It's general practice for our clients to offer terms to their customers. They would like to get paid right away, but that's not how it really works, right? When businesses offer their customers payment terms, it creates long payment cycles. They end up getting paid at all different times, making it very difficult for them to keep up with operational expenses in a timely manner.

Factoring is not a loan. It doesn't create additional debt. It gets you your money right away. When you sell your invoices and receive that cash on the faster than if you were able to use a credit card, you can more accurately predict and forecast your future supply needs. An immediate influx of cash allows them to leverage discounts from suppliers or buy larger quantities at reduced rates. We have numerous stories from our clients about how their business benefited from being able to make discounted purchases for things like fuel and other items, or get wholesale pricing.

There is strength in having cash in hand. Cash in hand is clout. It gives you the best options. People are more willing to listen to you and take you seriously when there is real dollars on the line. Factoring turns invoices into immediate cash. Our services quickly provide our clients with the necessary funds they need to stay operational. It eliminates the worry of waiting 30, 45 or 60-plus days for payment by providing them with working capital right away. They can meet payroll, pay suppliers and buy the things they need when they need them.

There are more benefits to factoring. It takes a lot of time to manage accounts receivable. This is time that could be spent on managing and growing your business but is tied up in paperwork and bookkeeping. Turning your accounts receivable over to a factoring firm frees up your time so you can focus on day-to-day operations and expanding your business. It can also put you in a position to offer your customers better terms. Offering better terms makes you more attractive and opens you up for better growth opportunities.

Questions

How are you managing your accounts receivable?

_____

_____

_____

_____

Have you considered factoring as an option?

_____

_____

_____

_____

"Cash is king."

Proverb

Chapter 15

Keep Adding Value

Our company is always in a state of evolution. So we are always asking ourselves what we need to evaluate. It's easy to get stuck, right? No company is impervious to that. A couple of sayings come to mind like "if it ain't broke, don't fix it", or "don't mess with a good thing". There does come a time when you have to listen to the market, look at your audience and re-evaluate. What does my audience look like now? Imagine it is 20 years later, and it's probably the same audience but they look different today than they did back then. They may have the same problems and you've got the same solutions, but now you've got to look at how to provide that solution in a better way, a way that brings value to how your client operates today.

Dorado's shortest tenure is eight years. That's the shortest time period that someone has been a part of our business and a part of our family. That's golden in business today. Our employees are our partners and we have total trust in our relationship. They know our business as well as we do. They are loyal and we know they have the company's best interest at heart in everything they do. So we must be doing something right..

That kind of stability is important to our long-term clients too. It means they work with the same person every time. They get to know them on a very personal level. They know about their families, their kids and their pets. There is an established level of trust and comfort in knowing that we've got their back. In every communication and every interaction that we have with our clients, we show them that we value them. You don't get that with larger companies or banks. It goes back to the partnerships we have with our employees and our clients. Again, it's about having those deep relationships.

But that's not the whole of it. Your client may have already re-invented itself to keep up with its market. It may have a new and younger generation of employees. That new generation brings different ideas and solutions to how your client is doing business. You have to keep up and understand who your client is now. It's about asking questions. Asking questions about how you are doing or how you can improve. Be prepared to listen to some answers that may be hard to listen to. And act on them. Don't just sweep them under the rug. The answers you get are going to help you add the right value in the right areas of your business.

Examine your niche in the market and what expertise you provide. Try to identify what you can do better or more effectively. What is your target audience looking for now? Develop your own system, for instance, a survey you can use to ask your clients where you can add value. Ask them about your performance. Ask them about their new needs. What changes and trends do they notice? I'll tell you right now that the problems they face today are very different from those 20 years ago, even 10 years ago. Technology has created and is continuing to force enormous changes in the way people conduct business now. Look at how the internet alone has created a new environment for consumers to do business…not to mention what machine learning will be doing in 10 years.

Many of the manually driven processes we used to do are now automated. Some of these changes have affected the way my clients do business. For example, we used to file everything in folders that were stored in large filing cabinets. Each piece of paper had to be manually put into a folder and filed in the right location. It could be quite a laborious task. Some large companies had rooms full of these cabinets just to store their records. And they needed someone to file the papers and manage the system. This created opportunity for my clients like H&H to offer staffing assistance. But now almost every document we create can be stored right on our computer or, if not on your computer, there is a whole storage service called the cloud.

Technological changes have made some of the services that were once provided by my clients obsolete. But it has also opened doors for them to provide new services and add value for their customers. There are new problems and differences in the way we all operate now as opposed to a few years ago. Look at your competitors. How are they adapting to the technology being used today? What does technology look like? When we look at that, we can see what options are available to us and we can better adapt to the changing environment.

Amazon is one of the greatest examples I can think for being able to adapt and stay relevant in today's ever-changing environment. They continuously learn, evolve and make themselves a better version of what they are today. It's not about lowering prices. They certainly have a range that any consumer can choose from depending on the product. And anyone can have a sale. What Amazon understands well is that competitive advantage is about being adaptable. Think about it. Amazon started out selling books and then became a logistics company and now its competing with SpaceX's rockets. You can buy practically anything you want and have it delivered right to your door overnight or sometimes within an hour. That's adaptability at its finest.

Different clients will also have distinctive problems associated with their type of business. For instance, we deal a lot with trucking companies and staffing companies. Although they are both service-oriented companies, their operations and the problems they face are unique. Therefore, we need to be able to provide unique solutions to the problems they experience in their industry. The value we bring to one will be different from the value we bring to the other. But it is value all the same.

Our clients are the lifeblood of our business. Without them, we aren't in business. We don't want them to just be satisfied. We want them to be delighted with the value they receive from doing business with our company. As I said earlier, our business thrives on word-of-mouth advertising. That advertising comes directly from our clients. And with the technology available today, that word-of-mouth review can spread far and wide. We are obligated to improve upon our service and continuously add value for our clients so that they can continue to add value to their customers. We are all in business to help others be in business.

It's your responsibility to keep evolving as you move forward. It's essential that your business is agile. You must learn to adapt to changing times so your business stays relevant. You need to be able to see the future before it happens and keep ahead of changing technology. The business landscape is always changing, and you need to stay ahead of the curve. If you don't keep up and modify your processes to changing environments, you will go out of business.

Create a system for regularly reaching out to your clients. Be proactive. Get in front of people. Everyone wants to do with business with companies that stay on the cutting edge. Keep abreast of what's happening. Continuously identify new opportunities that offer better solutions to your clients and keep adding value. Listen to your clients. Your clients will tell you what they see and what they want.

If you do all these things I've been writing about in this book, you will always be looking for value. You will automatically become a solution-oriented culture that continuously seeks to add value. You will establish an advantage over your competitors by being agile and getting ahead of the market. Your company continue to grow and stay relevant in the future. Your brand will become a symbol for solving problems while adding value for your clients.

Questions

Are you connecting with your target audience regularly?

_____

_____

_____

_____

How is technology in today's business environment affecting them?

_____

_____

_____

_____

When was the last time you asked your clients how you are doing?

_____

_____

_____

_____

Review the services you provide. How effective are they?

_____

_____

_____

_____

When was the last time you asked can you improve?
List three improvements you think you can make right now
that will add value for your clients.

_____

_____

_____

_____

_____

_____

_____

"Let's have some fun and make some money."

Gene Reddick

Acknowledgements

Our business is familia! It's all about family. If there isn't family, there isn't a business.

Christine Reddick. My mom is my rock. She has never not believed in everything I've done. She is my biggest advocate and has always been there for me. Best mom in the world.

Gene Reddick. My father influenced me beyond anyone else. His influence was huge. Every example of doing business came from him. My work ethic, how I work, how to do business and how to succeed all came from him. I learned how to be an entrepreneur from him.

Dick Daniel. My uncle was another big influence on me. He was very successful in finance and a beaming example of being humble.

Jason Crawford. Former CEO of IRIS. He exemplified leadership in a way that is unmatched. He taught me it was ok to make mistakes. We got to pioneer a company from nothing into something incredible.

Resources Recommended by the Author

- Dorado Finance – www.doradofinance.com
- SCORE Volunteer Mentors - www.score.org
- Superior Custom Pins – www.superiorcustompins.com
- HubSpot CRM – www.hubspot.com
- Elevate Marketing – www.whyelevate.com
- Heather DeSantis Public Relations – www.desantispr.com
- Trace Reddick – www.tracereddickmba.com